KOR Productions & Anna Doolan in association
with Rua Arts presents

T0190802

POISONED
POLLUTED

by Kathryn O'Reilly

Poisoned Polluted was first performed at the Old Red Lion Theatre,
Islington, on 5 November 2019.

POISONED POLLUTED

by Kathryn O'Reilly

CAST
Kathryn O'Reilly
Anna Doolan

CREATIVE TEAM

Director & Dramaturg	Lucy Allan
Movement Director	Sophie Shaw
Set & Costume Designer	Mayou Trikerioti
Lighting Designer	Benny Goodman
Sound Designer	Nicola Chang
Stage Manager	Hester Blindell
Press & Publicity	Chloe Nelkin Consultancy
Rehearsal & Production shots	Robert Workman
Promo Images	Nick Rutter
Flyer & Poster Design	Nick Thompson
Technician	Ryan Perry

PRODUCTION TEAM

Producers	Kathryn O'Reilly – KOR Productions
	Anna Doolan
	Maeve O'Neill – Rua Arts

SUPPORT
Funding has been gratefully received from The Carne Trust.

THE
CARNE TRUST
Supporting young talent in the performing arts

THANKS

Kathryn would like to thank

Patrick Morris at Junction Theatre Cambridge

Nick Hern, Matt Applewhite, Sarah Liisa Wilkinson, Jodi Gray

Neil Grutchfeild

Nadia Nadif

Carre

Mimi Findlay, Anna Herrmann and Clean Break

Martin Derbyshire and Kate Wasserberg at Out of Joint

Katy Danbury

Anna Doolan

Barry Wright

Grace Gummer

Hester Blindell, John Hill technical manager Rose Bruford College

Charlie O'Reilly

Rob Ogilvie, Croydon Youth Theatre

Jelena Budimir

Ignite Theatre

Philip and Christine Carne

Dylan and all at Old Red Lion

Nick Quinn and Alfie Coates at The Agency

Technical Manager Jonathan Hill

Scenic Arts Manager David Kerry, for support and equipment

BIOGRAPHIES

KATHRYN O'REILLY | SISTER | WRITER | PRODUCER
Kathryn trained at the National Youth Theatre, BRIT Performing Arts school and did a BA in drama at LAMDA.

Theatre credits include: *Skin in the Game* (Old Red Lion, Birmingham Fest - Best Performer Award); *Close Quarters* (Sheffield Crucible); *Our Country's Good* (St James, Bolton Octagon tour, Guthrie Theater Minneapolis, Royal Alexandra Toronto); *A View from Islington North* (Arts Theatre); *Andersen's English* (Hampstead Theatre/tour); *Mixed Up North* (Wilton's Music Hall/tour) all for Out of Joint. *Bluebird* (Space Theatre); *Rift* (Brewhouse Theatre); *Love on the Tracks* (Redbridge, Soho Theatre studio); *A Christmas Carol* (Trafalgar Studios); *Arms and the Man* (Watford Palace Theatre); *YOU* (Vault Festival - Show of the Week Award winners; Brighton Fringe, Argus Angel Award Winners); *The Golden Dragon* (ATC/Arcola); *Caught*, *hamlet is dead. no gravity* (Arcola).

Feature film credits include: *Rare Beasts* directed by Billie Piper; *The Little Stranger* directed by Lenny Abrahamson; *Zebra Crossing* (BIFA award winner). Short films include: *For Him* directed by Ian Killick; *Dazedly* directed by Anona Langa; *The Guard* directed by Shona Charlton; *Nation Your Nation* directed by Frederick Kell; *Klink Klank* directed by Robert Reina; *Cold Calling* directed by Jess Quinones - winner Best Comedy 2007 indi short.

Television: *Grantchester, Lewis* (ITV); *Call the Midwife, Holby City, Doctors* (BBC); *The Bill* (Talkback Thames;, *Rough Justice* (Hewland Int); *The Watcher* (UFA Fiction); BAFTA award-winning TV film *random* written and directed by debbie tucker-green.

As a writer Kathryn was a member of the Royal Court Young Writers' Programme, completed playwriting courses at CIty Lit, and is currently studying at Essex University.

Her debut play *Screwed* premiered at Theatre503 and is published by Nick Hern Books. Whilst at LAMDA she won the original poetry writing competition two years consecutively.

Rehearsed readings of her work include *Severed* at Soho Theatre directed by Jelena Budimir (cast - Maggie Steed, Joanna Bacon, Barbara Peirson, Linda Clark); *Scarred* at Out of Joint - directed by Blanche McIntyre (cast - Carey Mulligan, Johnny Harris, Phil Davis, Jamie Foreman, Emma Lowndes, Mattew Needham) and *Klink Klank Echoes* at Tristan Bates directed by Hannah Eidinow (cast - Gary Carr, Eloise Joseph, Anthony Welsh, Kathryn O'Reilly). www. kathryn-oreilly.com

As a producer Kathryn is a StageOne alumni and for her production company KOR Productions has produced *Screwed* (Theatre503) and short film *Caught*.

Other theater includes *Semblance of Madness!* (Etcetera Theatre); *Not About Heroes* (Baron's Court); *Little Shop of Horrors, Top The Pops, The Nutcracker, Blood Brothers* (Lewisham Theatre Studio).

Kathryn has also produced staged readings of her own work and Andrew Cartmel's *Screwball* at Jermyn Street Theatre directed by Conrad Blakemore, and the short film *Klink Klank* as well as her own music and word events at Tea House Theatre and Tristan Bates Theatre with Tas Emiabata with whom she has an EP called *Rising*.

ANNA DOOLAN | HER | PRODUCER
Training: Guildford School of Acting BA (Hons) Acting 2006-2009

Theatre credits include: *Mighty Atoms* directed by Mark Babych (Hull Truck); *Bluebird* (The Space); *Wesley* directed by Jimmy Grimes (The Avenue); *Dreamers: This Property is Condemned* by Tennessee Williams (New End/Hackney Empire studio); *And a Nightingale Sang* (The New Vic/Stephen Joseph/Oldham Coliseum); *Comedy of Errors,Wuthering Heights* (Theatre in the Forest – Jimmy's Farm); *The Magic Fishbone* (Christchurch Mansion/Theatre in the Forest – Jimmy's Farm); *The Accrington Pals* (Fairfield Halls/The Pomegranate Theatre); *Dracula* (Fairfield Halls); *The Big Sleep, Joking Apart* by Alan Ayckbourn (The Mill at Sonning).

Short film credits include: *Caught* directed by Fredrick Kelly; *Penance* directed by Steven Arnold; *Sometimes a Fantasy* directed by Lee Howard (Canned Films); *Street Girl* directed by Lee Howard (Super 8 series); *Custody* directed by Steven Arnold (Canned Media); *Desire* directed by Leon Ockenden (Giddy Kipper Films).

Television credits: *The Hour* (BBC/KUDOS).

Music videos credits: Lucinda Belle – 'Where have all the good men gone', John Turner (Passion Pictures); Javeon – 'Mercy' directed by Ben Strebel; 'Vienna in Love' directed by Robert Johnston.

Commercial credits include: Cadburys, Blac Ionica, Tim Wetherall, Jon Evans, Chris Strong. HELLO.IE, Ben Dodd (Space City); NHS, WORTH TALKING ABOUT (COI); Orange phones, Ohav (Castel Films).

Producer credits : *Caught* (short film).

LUCY ALLAN | DIRECTOR | DRAMATURG
Lucy was trainee director at Leeds Playhouse from 2018-2019. She is co-artistic director of award-winning theatre company Unholy Mess.

Training: Theatre Directing MFA, Birkbeck 2017–2019.

Directing credits include: *Above the Mealy-Mouthed Sea* (international tour); *Melody* (national tour); *Unsung* (The Rosemary Branch/Wilton's Music Hall); *Can't Stand Up for Falling Down* (Studio Salford, The Lowry Studio); *Rootbound, Rigor Mortis* (The Miniaturists at the Arcola).

Assisting credits include: *Around the World in 80 Days, Hamlet, Dinner 18:55, Kes* (Leeds Playhouse); *Not Such Quiet Girls* (Opera North); *Airplays* (BBC Radio Leeds); *The Shawshank Redemption* (Assembly Rooms); *Cyrano de Bergerac* (Grosvenor Park Open Air Theatre).

SOPHIE SHAW | MOVEMENT DIRECTOR

Sophie trained in Dance and Drama at Winchester University. She completed a PGCE at Central School of Speech and Drama and started to understand what real collaborative work was while teaching in an East London secondary school. After leaving full-time teaching she set up a Community Interest Company that worked with marginalised groups – running creative projects for vulnerable adults as well as young people at risk of underachievement in school. During this time Sophie worked freelance for a variety of theatre companies including Freshwater Theatre Company (performer); Clean Break Theatre Company (movement direction and teaching) and began working for Frantic Assembly in 2017 as a practitioner. She is Associate Movement Director on the schools tour of *The Curious Incident of the Dog in the Night-Time*, and before that, assisted with movement direction in the 2018 West End version at the Piccadilly Theatre. She is proud to have co-directed the first (pilot) female Ignition. Since finishing an MA in Devised Theatre and Performance at Berlin Arthaus, she is enjoying working as a freelancer and collaborating in a range of different creative projects.

MAYOU TRIKERIOTI | SET & COSTUME DESIGNER

Mayou trained at the Bristol Old Vic Theatre School after finishing her BA honours in Drama and Theatre Studies at the University of Kent. Mayou has been working mostly in Greece and the UK and has worked with major theatres and festivals including the National Theatre in Athens, the Ancient theatre of Epidavros, the Young Vic, the Rose, the Garrick and the Harold Pinter Theatres. She works on all scales grand and small, and her portfolio ranges from plays that enjoyed successful runs of two+ years to one-off, site-specific performances and from West End shows to fringe gems. Since 2007 Mayou has been designing feature and short films that have traveled across the globe and screened at international film festivals, including Venice Film Festival, Berlin and Toronto IFF. Mayou also enjoys working on community art projects that engage local youth and residents. She is one of the founding members and co-artistic directors of Change of Art, a community arts project created by a group of theatre practitioners and artists, who came together through shared activism. For further information and current projects please visit: www.mayoutrikerioti.com

NICOLA CHANG | SOUND DESIGN

Nicola is a composer/sound designer for theatre, film and commercial media across the UK, US and Asia. As a performer, she currently plays for *Six* (West End) as Dep Keys/Musical Director and she is a former cast member of *STOMP!* (West End/world tur). She is also an Artistic Associate of the King's Head Theatre and a BFI x BAFTA Crew Member. She has performed at the Royal Albert Hall, the Royal Festival Hall and the Shakespeare's Globe as a percussionist, and holds a MMus in Composition from King's College London. Additionally, she is a composer and musical director attached to British Youth Music Theatre UK. Her theatre credits include: *The Ice Cream Boys* (Jermyn Street); *Little Baby Jesus, The Tempest* (Orange Tree); *Wild Goose Dreams* (Theatre Royal Bath); *Germ Free Adolescent* (Bunker); *The King of Hell's Palace* (Hampstead); *The Death of Ophelia* (Sam Wanamaker Playhouse, Shakespeare's Globe); *Summer Rolls* (Park); *White Pearl* (Royal Court); *From Shore to Shore* (Royal Exchange Theatre, Manchester/UK tour); *Lord of the Flies* (Greenwich); *Dangerous Giant Animals* (Tristan Bates); *Finishing the Picture* (Finborough); *A Hundred Words for Snow* (Arcola) and *The Free9* (National Theatre). www.nicolatchang.com

BENNY GOODMAN | LIGHTING DESIGN

Benny is a freelance lighting designer and creative collaborator, based in Glasgow and London. Benny studied Lighting Design at the Royal Conservatoire of Scotland, also receiving the Simon Crowther Award for Excellence and Commitment to the Institution. Since graduating, he has been working in theatres across the UK in a variety of projects and productions, and is a creative collaborator with the theatre company, Wonder Fools. Selected credits include: *The Drift* (National Theatre of Scotland); *Like Animals, The Afflicted* (Summerhall); *Act of Repair* (Scottish Youth Theatre national tour); *Country Music* (Omnibus); *549: Scots of the Spanish Civil War* (Wonder Fools UK tour); *The Mistress Contract* (Tron); *Daddy Drag* (Assembly Roxy); *Where We Are: The Mosque* (Arcola); *Sorella Mia* (The Place, London); *Birthright, Good Women, Blue Departed* (VAULT Festival, London); *Disarming Reverberations* (St Giles Cathedral, Edinburgh); *Heroines* (BBC Alba, Stornoway); *Humbug* (Tramway, Glasgow); *Snow Queen* (Associate – RCS/Dundee Rep Theatre); *Like Animals, The Poetry House* (Tron Theatre); *Ayanfe Opera* (Bridewell, London) *Wired* (Summerhall, Edinburgh); Immaculate Correction (King's Head, London); *Sideshow* (West Brewery, Glasgow); *The Coolidge Effect* (Tron/Traverse/Glasgow School of Art); *Spring Awakening* (Associate – RCS/Dundee Rep); *549:Scots of the Spanish Civil War, Lampedusa, Pleasure and Pain* (Citizens); *Circle of Fifths* (Tron/Cockpit). For further information on his work www.bennygoodman.co

HESTER BLINDELL | STAGE MANAGER

Hester is currently in her third year of the Stage and Events Management degree at Rose Bruford College of Performance Arts. She also studied performance related courses for two years at Clean Break. Credits as a stage manager: *Constance and Kelly* (Waiting in the Dark Theatre) at Bloomsbury Theatre and Rose Bruford. Deputy Stage Manager: *Lydia Osborne* (Rose Bruford MA Devised) at Shoreditch Town Hall, *Digit[All]* (Rose Bruford ETA Devised); *Let Me Shake Your Groove Thing* (Wardrobe Ensemble) at The Ugly Duck. Assistant Stage Manager: *The Secret Garden* (Urdang Academy) at Bernie Grants Arts Centre, Showcase (Urdang Academy) at Hackney Empire.

RUA ARTS | PRODUCER

Rua, an Irish word meaning red; the colour of blood, energy and life. Rua Arts offers project management, arts administration and mentoring for artists and arts organisations led by arts producer, Maeve O'Neill. Maeve is an independent arts producer, specialising in artist-led producing and mentoring. Maeve has managed productions, national tours and participation projects for artists, theatre companies and arts organisations including; Apples & Snakes, Roundhouse, Ovalhouse, Daedalus Theatre and NIE Theatre. She produced the premier of Blind Summit's award-winning show, *The Table* at The Pleasance for Edinburgh Festival Fringe 2011 and two national tours of *The Diary of a Hounslow Girl* by Ambreen Razia with Black Theatre Live and House Theatre. Other credits include: *POT* by Ambreen Razia (Ovalhouse/national tour); *Friends For All* (national tour) and *Mole & Gecko: The Show* (national tour) by Simon Mole; *Screwed* by Kathryn O'Reilly (Theatre503); *Hidden* by Nicola Werenowska (regional tour) and *The Reverse Is Also True* by Stephen May (national tour). Maeve originally trained at Gaiety School of Acting, Dublin and completed a BA in Modern Drama Studies at Brunel University. www.ruaarts.earth

POISONED POLLUTED

Kathryn O'Reilly

Characters

HER
SISTER

*This text went to press before the end of rehearsals and so may
differ slightly from the play as performed.*

Movement – moments from movement sections later in the play.

HER *twenty-three*. SISTER *twenty-eight*.

HER	You look –
SISTER	Yeah –
HER	Great.
SISTER	Thank you.
HER	Never seen you look so good. Really. Really.
SISTER	Alright.
HER	I didn't think –
SISTER	What?
HER	No, I don't mean…
SISTER	Didn't didn't believe in me?
HER	No, I'm not saying that.
SISTER	No.
HER	You know I'm not saying that. I'm proud of you.
SISTER	Oh. Why didn't you just say that?
HER	I am. You should be proud of yourself.
SISTER	Yeah.
HER	How long have you got this for?
SISTER	Erm… two years maybe.
HER	That's good.
SISTER	If I'm a good girl, and don't don't break any of the rules, don't fail any of their tests.
HER	Shall I make us a drink?

SISTER	I haven't got a kettle yet.
HER	Should have told me I could have bought you a kettle.
SISTER	I don't want you to buy me a kettle.
HER	Well I won't buy you a kettle.
SISTER	I told you it wasn't ready, this place isn't ready.
HER	That's a television.
SISTER	Don't don't touch it. I'm waiting for the box.
HER	It's massive.
SISTER	Doesn't work yet.
HER	That's like having your own cinema. I know where I'll be watching a film when I'm back.
SISTER	I won't be in.
HER	It's great to see you... looking so healthy.
SISTER	Funny, all I ate was Richmond sausages and drank copious amounts of coffee, instant shit with sugar. We were told it was normal coffee with caffeine in it. It wasn't.
HER	I've put weight on.
SISTER	Yeah I know.
HER	Thank you. Nick doesn't mind.
SISTER	Nick?
HER	Nick.

Beat.

| SISTER | It was good to get away from everything. |
| HER | You're telling me. I felt like I was on holiday with you there, I knew exactly where you were and what you were doing. Let's go out. We could go for a walk. |

SISTER   I don't don't want to go for a walk.

HER   I don't think you should be cooped up in here.

SISTER   I don't don't think you need to tell me what I should and shouldn't be doing. They showed us this video one session, group session, an animation of a ship out at sea, it was really shit the animation, and all these ghouls and ghosts and monsters and creatures were trying to get up the side of the ship and on the ship and drown it. And that's what this is. You need to get off my ship.

HER   Get off your ship?

SISTER   Don't take the piss.

HER   I'm not.

SISTER   You think you are better than me.

HER   ...No I don't.

SISTER   You had it better than me that's for sure. I've had a lot of time to think about things.

HER   That's good, that's really good.

SISTER   Had time to talk about things, like talk about things...

HER   That's great.

SISTER   Is it?

           Shit happened before you were born that you don't know about.

HER   Like what?

SISTER   Like I don't want to talk about it right now.

HER   Okay.

           Beat.

           Things happened to me too.

SISTER   Yeah, well I didn't have a big sister looking out for me protecting me.

HER   No.

SISTER   Right.

I get these recurring... recurring feelings. And I see it vividly a gaunt dark figure, eyes rolled back. Always lingering, looming over me. My back tenses up, shoulders hunch up, fists clench, stomach tightens, chest out, and I can't breathe can't move, there's something behind me, and in front of me. Everything is held with so much tension I think I might break my back my shoulders my fists stomach and chest might just break. I hear a crack. My clenched fist loosens. The momentum drags me down. There's the tapping a light tapping, a suction and I can't move anything, can't breathe I'm sweating, I'm grappling for oxygen, then a gust of wind fills my lungs and I float one two three I'm in a better place, floating.

Silence.

HER *six*. SISTER *eleven*.

HER   You're eleven. I'm six.
Today.
I'm six.

SISTER   Sat around the kitchen table.
Party Rings, chocolate cake, cheesy Wotsits, paper plates and tissue hats. Pass-the-Parcel, fizzy pop and her, Mum standing staring at me leaning against the sink, back door open, smoking, chain-smoking, drinking her adult pop and pausing the music. Laughing.

HER   I was allowed five friends. Only two came. Cheryl and her sister.

SISTER   Yeah we all laughed. Every time the music stopped and someone ripped a layer of paper off the parcel with excited delight only to find a chocolate coin or even better nothing. It was hilarious. She was like 'ahhhh', 'ooooh' like there was something amazing in the centre, and it felt like we were building up to something really really really fun.

And wrapped inside the last layer – finally – in the centre – the winner –

HER   Which wasn't me.

SISTER   Wasn't you. She, Mum could of rigged it but she didn't didn't – the winner, me, the winner found a collection of plastic shit.
Nothing exciting or fun or amazing, just shit.
Plastic red dice
plastic green frog
a yellow plastic saw.
I looked at her and she looked at the ground.
Just a load of junk that she'd saved from the Christmas crackers.
Well I'll give her credit for being green.

HER   My new party dress was for age ten-plus.

SISTER   That'll see you for the next four birthdays.

HER   That would be funny if it wasn't sad.

SISTER   I think she was trying.

HER   Obviously got it when she was out of it. Either that or she forgot how old I was. Probably both.
The party is over and Cheryl and her sister have gone home.

SISTER   I hear a tapping and our mum sat now, slouching in a chair by the open back door.

HER   We played Blind Man's Buff with our dad.

SISTER   Spin him faster.

HER   Yeah!

SISTER   Yeeeaaahh. We will. We will spin you faster.

HER   Yeah!

               HER laughing. They both spin their imaginary father around, faster, laughing excitedly. Backing away as he falls about, dizzy, they jump away from his arms as he searches for them. Lost in enjoyment.

SISTER   Get her.

HER   Ssshhh. No, no, no, no, no, no, no, no don't get me.

SISTER   Get her. Daddy get her.

               Movement – SISTER, *playful, runs around to get away from the dad, screams and laughs as she is 'got'.*

HER   He gropes in the air, feeling his way. We dodge but he grabs my sister, tickles her. Hands over her body.

SISTER   That tickles, that tickles.

               SISTER *goes into slow-motion movement of her father tickling her, she's laughing.*

HER   Maybe she saw it as well from the back door.
Maybe she knew.
She didn't say anything about it if she did, didn't do anything.
She was jealous of him playing with us because she didn't know how to.
Because he liked us more than he liked her.
And we liked him more than we liked her.
And she didn't even like herself.

               SISTER *comes out of slow-motion movement.*

               He took the blindfold off. His eyes gleaming looking at us both. Breathy heavy laughing.
Mum tries to get up, or, she slowly slumps down even more in her chair, she'll fall off the chair and crack her head on the floor. I rush towards her I hug her and then she's sick, she pukes up right down my dress. Crumples to the floor.

HER *screams, frozen on the spot, looking down at
the dress, her shoes.*

SISTER   Take it off.

HER   I can't.

SISTER   Take it off.

HER   Smells disgusting.

SISTER   Take it off.

HER   I can't touch it.

SISTER   Yes you can.

          Yeah! We'll take ours off.

HER   Then he took off his shirt.
          Throws it on the floor.
          He's topless. Hairy, thick dark hairs, wet with sweat.
          Beckoning my sister, 'arms up', he takes her dress
          off, over her head, he throws it on top of his shirt.
          They both turn and stare at me.
          I took off my party dress for age ten-plus with her
          sick, and threw it on the floor where she lies
          moaning. I want to wipe the sick off my shoes on her
          face. I want to kick her face, but Dad starts chasing
          my sister again. She's screaming with laughter.
          Running around me in her knickers and long socks
          and shoes.
          I kick my shoes off.
          I'm piggy in the middle, and I smell him, his sweat,
          deodorant, alcohol. Remember watching how his
          arms moved, the muscles in his back.
          He grabs her, laughs, swings her around, lifts her up
          and slowly slides her down his chest, skin to skin.
          She's dizzy. She falls and he gets down on the floor
          with her, hand on her leg.
          Then dresses her with his shirt. She gets up with his
          shirt on and he pats her bottom and she laughs, and
          he does it again, and she laughs and he does it again
          and she spins round showing off the dress shirt.

SISTER   I've got a new dress. I've got a new dress.

HER   Our mum has been lying there motionless for ages
            then suddenly drags herself up moaning – stops
            the music.
            We don't care it was her music anyway.
            She stumbles to the fridge, slams the door, opens
            another drink.
            And drops it on the floor. Thud.
            He grabs me – grabs us – pretending to protect us
            from her, holds us very close, very tight, squashing
            us, I can feel him.
            I wait for him to let go I step back and my sister
            holds on to him.
            Mum swipes at the can on the floor pouring
            everywhere, staggers towards us, eyes full of
            hatred, pupils so small, staggers closer then treads
            on the sick, on her own sick on my dress and slips,
            lands on the floor with a big thud and Dad and my
            sister laugh.
            We laugh together.
            At her.
            Hugging Dad's shirt close to her as she laughs.
            I've never seen her laugh so much.
            Not before and not since.

            *SISTER is laughing so much, and parades around
            HER in the shirt.*

            *Suddenly from out of nowhere, the imaginary mum
            grabs at HER leg and tries to pull her down.
            SISTER jumps straight in front of HER in
            protection mode.*

SISTER   No. No. No. No. No. No. No. No. Leave her alone.

            *The mum viciously tries to lash out and gets up.
            She slaps SISTER right across the legs. The sting
            of the slap makes SISTER take a deep breath,
            incredulous. Time slows down. Slow-motion
            movement and no audible dialogue as SISTER gets*

slapped in the face, she kicks back. HER *is mouthing a scream at the mum: 'We hate you, we hate you, we hate you.'*

Early spring morning, birds singing their mating song outside.

HER *puts make-up on* SISTER – *a split lip, scratch marks on her legs and* SISTER *puts a bruise across* HER *face.*

SISTER *creeps up on* HER *and pinches her arm.*

Pinch, punch, first day of the month and no return.

HER	Ow!
SISTER	Sshh. Don't be a baby.
HER	I'm not a baby.
SISTER	Spring baby.
HER	What time is it?
SISTER	Time to get up. I love spring.
HER	Yeah?
SISTER	It's my favourite season. Days are longer.
HER	How can days be longer?
SISTER	It gets warmer.
HER	How can days be longer?
SISTER	They just are. Animals come out of hibernation. What's your favourite season?
HER	I don't know.
SISTER	Be like me. I don't mind. You can have spring as your favourite season too.
HER	Okay. Yeah. Spring.
SISTER	Haven't you done a project yet, on spring? In spring the leaves become green, butterflies dance, hedgehogs and bats come out of hibernation –

HER   Bats?

SISTER   Yeah, and the birds sing their mating songs.

HER   Mating songs.

SISTER   Yeah, fucking, birds fuck too.

             HER *gasps in shock.*

             Dad told me, took me to the forest and listened to
             the fucking birds.

HER   Birds do that?

SISTER   Do what?

HER   What you just said.

SISTER   What did I say?

HER   The word beginning with F.

SISTER   What word?

HER   F'ff –

SISTER   F'ff fudge cakes.

HER   No.

SISTER   F'ff fiddlesticks.

HER   No.

SISTER   F'ff flippin' flapping floppy flabby fruit cakes.

HER   You said fuck.

             SISTER *mockingly gasps at* HER.

             You did.

SISTER   Yeah – I did I said fuckfuckfuckfuckfuckfuckfuck
             and everything changes.

             SISTER *starts quietly whistling a tune like a bird.*
             HER *joins in. They giggle quietly. The whistling
             noise continues under this dialogue, starts to echo
             hauntingly.*

HER   Why's it so quiet?

SISTER   I don't know.

HER   Maybe Mum will stay in bed again for another
            week.

SISTER   Yeah moaning. Uuurrggh my body aches,
            uuurrgggh my legs, uuurrgggh I'm going to be sick
            uuurrgggh.

HER   Maybe she lost her memory –

SISTER   Yeah maybe she fell out of bed and cracked her
            head and blood is trickling out of her head and
            seeping into the floorboards – Maybe she's
            sleepwalking somewhere with a broken head and
            people are pointing at her and staring and laughing.
            And maybe she walks off a bridge.

            Maybe they've run away. Left us, and we are all
            alone. Let's go. Downstairs.

HER   Maybe she lost her memory.

SISTER   Maybe Dad's killed her. Kicked her head in. Pulled
            her eyes out and is going to eat them for breakfast,
            like boiled eggs.

HER   Shall we have chocolate cake for breakfast?

SISTER   Yeah, chocolate cake toast sandwich.

HER   Shall we!

SISTER   Yeah.

HER   Yes! Mmmm.

SISTER   Sshhh.

HER   What?

SISTER   I like it when it's just me and you, the two of us
            and the house is quiet.

HER   We creep into the kitchen as quietly as we can.

            Bread in the toaster. Quietly down. Click.

            SISTER *turns, sees Mum on the floor and freezes.*

Creep open the rubber seal on the fridge door slight suction pop.

SISTER   Mum?

HER   There's not enough.

SISTER   What are you doing on the floor?

HER   They've been eating my birthday cake.

SISTER   Mum.

HER   They said, she said she was saving it.

SISTER   GET UP!

HER   The cardboard with half a slice of birthday cake slid out of my hands.
Light thud on the floor makes me jump. I laugh.

SISTER   What – stop laughing.

HER   Why is she sleeping on the floor?

SISTER *bends down carefully to inspect.*

SISTER   What the what the what the –

HER   Sleeping Lions.

SISTER   She's not shut up she's not what why why is she doing why are you why are you why are you why are you w fr w f f f why are you freezing cold?

HER   Mum!

SISTER   W w w w wake up, wake up, wake up, wake up.

HER   My sister tried to turn our mum over, as she tried she fell back.

SISTER   Wake up wake up wake up now.

HER   And I was caught in her pinpoint pupils.
Startling.
Shock struck through her veins.
Stopped stock-still in her tracks.

Silence.

SISTER   Lips are purple.
           Stop staring. Say something. It's not funny. It's not
           funny.

HER   What's that around her arm?

SISTER   Why why why why why are you doing this? I told
           you stop doing this.

           Sound of the mum's last breath.

HER   Then she ran.

SISTER   Run.

HER   She ran out the back door, dragging me with her.
           Left at the end of our road. Right. To the end of that
           road past our school we kept running.
           She was usually way ahead of me. I could never
           challenge her to a race not normally. This morning
           I was running by her side, we were running together.
           We didn't stop until we got there.
           And when we got there we walked straight past the
           play area.
           To the forest.
           Everything was louder. Sounds of the breeze in the
           leaves. Sounds of flies and insects. And birds
           singing. Loudly.

           Pause.

           I'm hungry.

           Pause.

           Can we go now?

           Pause.

           I'm really really hungry.

           Pause.

           We might starve to death?

SISTER   Yeah, that can happen.

HER   What? What do you mean?

             SISTER *pretends with a twig to stab it in her arm
             and flail around dying, gurgling noises, reaching
             out for* HER *as* SISTER *pretends to die on the
             ground. This goes on for a little while and* HER
             *joins in, laughing. Sound of birds' mating songs
             comes back, louder this time.*

SISTER   Fucking birds.

HER   What?

SISTER   Birds and the bees and the flies in the trees. Shut up!

             Pause.

HER   Wish we had some macaroni cheese.

SISTER   I could go.

HER   Where?

SISTER   And get some.

             Beat.

HER   We can eat acorns I think.

SISTER   No we can't.

HER   Yeah we can.

SISTER   No we can't.

HER   Yeah we can.

SISTER   No we can't – Go on then.

HER   I don't want one.

SISTER   Go on.

HER   I don't want one.

             SISTER *picks up an acorn, holds it out to* HER.

SISTER   Eat one.

HER   No.

SISTER   Eat one.

HER   No.

SISTER   EAT ONE.

SISTER *thrusts it towards* HER *mouth.* HER *refuses.* SISTER *throws the acorn away and begins to walk off.*

HER   Don't leave me. I'll eat one. I'll eat one.

HER *picks up another acorn, just as* HER *gets it close to her mouth,* SISTER *grabs the acorn and throws it at the birds in the trees.*

SISTER   You can't eat acorns they are poisonous.

SISTER *gathers more acorns and throws them, aiming for birds in the trees.*

Birds and the bees and the flies in the trees. Shut. Them. Up. Shutupshutupshutupshutup.

HER *screams at the birds.* SISTER *screams.*

Beat.

Look at that.

HER   What?

SISTER   Don't move, look at that. They dig holes in one place, pretend to hide their acorns and cover the hole back up. Baffling other squirrels who go digging the hole, and they find there's nothing there. Just an empty hole.

In the meantime the clever one secretly squirrels away someplace safer when no other squirrel is looking. Leaves a scent track for themselves and buries their treasure only they know where. Cunning.

Ssshh, don't move.

Running. Jumping – some squirrels can fly.
Powerful paws propel themselves up up up.
Whoa, upside down what –

SISTER, *totally captivated, tries to entice the*
squirrel. Carefully she creeps forward towards the
squirrel. HER *is frozen on the spot.*

It's looking at me.

HER   It might bite you.

SISTER   Look at his eyes. Big and black and deep as
           a never-ending hole. You're amazing.

           They can see everything behind them, and what's
           in front of them.

HER   It might jump on you.

SISTER   I'm not scared.

HER   It's looking at me now.

SISTER   She won't hurt you.

HER   I will.

SISTER   It wants to play with us.

           SISTER *laughing. Like a cat-and-mouse game*
           between HER *and the squirrel,* SISTER *mimics the*
           squirrel's movements, she becomes the squirrel and
           darts back and forth, then jumps at HER.

HER   Get it off / get it off –

SISTER   It's just playing. It's okay. Don't be a baby.

HER   I'M NOT A BABY.

           The squirrel runs off.

SISTER   Look what you've done.

HER   I don't like it here any more.

SISTER   So fast. Imagine that, right to the treetop, zoom like
           that. They are protected.

HER	I'm cold. I want to go home now.
SISTER	This is our home now. Just us two. We can do whatever we want now. We can sleep in the trees. We have to stick together.
HER	Yeah.
SISTER	Always.
HER	Always.
SISTER	Yeah.
HER	You're my favourite.
SISTER	You're my favourite.
HER	More than what?
SISTER	You're my favourite more than macaroni cheese.
HER	You're my favourite more than all the teddy bears in the world.
SISTER	You're my favourite more than Freddos.
HER	You're my favourite forever.
SISTER	You're my favourite forever more than anything ever. I would save your life.
HER	From what?
SISTER	Anything. I would die for you.

SISTER *hugs* HER *close as they walk.*

If squirrels get cold, they can wrap their tails
around themselves and they have a blanket.
We could live here easily, like the sq–

SISTER, *frozen, has spotted Dad.*

Live like the squirrels in the trees.

HER	People chase them.

SISTER   No.

HER   Hunt them.

SISTER   No.

HER   Trap them.

SISTER   No.

HER   People hate them.

SISTER   I hate people.

HER   He found us. He came and found us in the forest.
We used to call it the forest. It wasn't a forest, it
was just the part of the park on the edge of the play
area that had a few oak trees in a line.

Is he crying?

*Movement – Two weeks pass. Everything changes.
The absence of Mum. Grief. Neglect. The funeral.*

It was a windy morning.
Hair all in my face.
Could hear the leaves in the trees.
The sound of the rope running through the gloves
of the men lowering the coffin down.
Dad threw some dirt, handed me dirt I threw some
dirt, thud on the coffin in the hole.
My sister stood there staring. She refused to throw
any dirt.
The wind blew.
The three of us sat in silence in the car on the
way back.
He gave up on everything. We hadn't been going to
school. My sister looked after me, and him. Social
Services came round to take us away and told us
we can bring one toy each. My sister got her
drawing pad and felt-tips, and stuffed her Secret
Squirrel pencil case in her pocket and put a big
jumper on. I had all my teddies lined up in height
order along my bed. I chose the one in the middle,
the yellow one.

My sister picked up my smallest teddy stuffed in
her other pocket under her jumper.
We went from one home to another. No one could
cope with us.
Then we went to Heather. We had our own
bedrooms. She was really good to us, I still had
nightmares though.
First time I wet the bed at Heather's I was so
petrified.

SISTER   I wet the bed. Her bed. She didn't do it. I did it.
I was in her room. It was me, hit me.

HER   Heather said it didn't matter, and put a plastic sheet
on the mattress.
Every year for my birthday Heather bought me
a new dress. Let me choose. Seventh, eighth, ninth,
tenth. I kept them all in my wardrobe even though
I was too big for most of them.

HER *fourteen*. SISTER *nineteen*.

Are you planning on running away?

SISTER   No. Why would I do that?

HER   I've seen you go out late at night.

SISTER   You should be asleep late at night.

HER   Have you got a boyfriend?

SISTER   None of your business.

HER   I saw you steal Heather's car.

SISTER   No you didn't.

HER   Can you drive me to the shops?

SISTER   What for?

HER   I need to get something special to wear for the
party.

SISTER   What party?

HER   It's fancy-dress.

SISTER   What do you need something new for? Just go as
             yourself.

HER   I'm telling Heather.

SISTER   You wouldn't dare.

HER   You haven't even got a licence.

SISTER   You don't even know anything.
             Mum used to let me drive. I used to hold the
             steering wheel – change gears. We'd drop you off
             at nursery, then I went out with Mum, spent the day
             with her. Didn't even go to school some days.
             Anyway I'm just trying to save Heather money
             when she finally pays for my driving lessons.

HER   Can you drive me?

SISTER   No.

HER   You're not invited anyway.

SISTER   I don't want to go anyway.

HER   You're not invited.

SISTER   Whose party is it anyway?

HER   It's Tom's.

SISTER   Tom?

HER   You don't know him, he's in my year.

SISTER   Is he your boyfriend?

HER   No.

SISTER   Has my little sister got a little boyfriend?

HER   No.

SISTER   Have you held hands?

HER   No.

SISTER   Ahhh.

HER   Cheryl's sister drives her in her car.

SISTER   Well ask Cheryl's sister.

HER   You're so annoying.

            Anyway I've snogged Tom already.

SISTER   You better not have.

HER   I hadn't. But I did that night at the fancy-dress
            party and I snogged a girl called Faith at the same
            party then I got drunk, smoked weed. Heather
            phoned me up to say she was picking me up and
            I told her I was staying out all night, she said she
            was coming and I swore at her and we had an
            argument and I ran away.
            For a night.
            Ran to my best friend Cheryl's house to see if
            I could stay there. Her mum answered the door and
            I went in.
            She made us bacon sandwiches on Mighty White
            as I ate my last mouthful the doorbell rang.
            I looked at Cheryl, she looked at me with a sorry
            face, I scowled at her and her mum, and when
            Heather marched me out I hissed back told Cheryl
            she wasn't my best friend any more.
            Heather ushered me into the back of the car. It was
            just a stupid argument we had.
            And my sister was there in the back too with a face
            so sad. Drove home in the dark in the silence.

SISTER   Is that cider I can smell?

HER   I felt a twinge in my heart.
            I could feel my sister looking at me and I couldn't
            look at her.
            I just thought I should jump out of the car now
            and run.
            I turned to the door, reached for the handle. Pulled
            the handle.

SISTER   Child lock's on. Because you are a child.

            HER *eighteen*. SISTER *twenty-three*.

            Human beings have the propensity for greatness.

HER	Who said that?
SISTER	Someone great.
HER	I don't know.
SISTER	Your perception of your life right now is too limited. You shouldn't deny yourself a great opportunity to expand your... your experience of living in its fullness. Do not let your mind deceive you. We have the potential to do anything, be literally anything.
HER	Have you been converted to... anything?
SISTER	What? No. Yeah yeah yeah I have yeah, been converted to the... understanding the possibility of... possibility.
HER	Possibility.
SISTER	But you have to believe it's possible.
HER	What?
SISTER	Anything. Change.
HER	Change is possible.
SISTER	Right. What we have is now. And tomorrow we have a different now. But if you don't go forward, what are you doing? So you should do it. Do it now. Wish I had of done it earlier.
HER	You were waiting for me.
SISTER	Exactly, yeah, I've been waiting for you.
HER	That's because I'm your favourite person ever.
SISTER	More than anything ever.
HER	More than what?
SISTER	More than... anything. Give yourself a chance. You can audit lectures on subjects you're not even studying. It's great. You can't live with Heather your whole life you know.

HER   Maybe I want to live with Heather my whole life.

SISTER   One day she'll say you've got to move out I've got
               new girls coming.

HER   She won't.

SISTER   She might. You're clever. You just don't want to
               know it.

HER   I'm only going to get two A levels, hardly you am I.

SISTER   Two A levels is amazing. You can do what you
               want. You can be great, if you want to.

HER   I might be pregnant.

               Silence.

SISTER   Great.

HER   Yeah.

SISTER   Yeah! That's great.

HER   Yeah.

SISTER   Yeah get a council flat.

               Summer.

               HER *nineteen.* SISTER *twenty-four.*

HER   What was she wearing?

SISTER   Do you remember when you were bang into clogs?
               You couldn't even walk properly. Hear you a mile
               off. I was like no I'm not her sister.

HER   There was a trend after I started wearing them.

SISTER   What of burning wood.

HER   You're not funny.

SISTER   No but you looked it.

HER   You're just jealous – I've always been trendy.

               HER *phone beeps with an alert.*

One hour left and these could be mine, what do you think?

SISTER   One hundred pounds for a sparkly pair of boots.

HER   Yeah, but I like them.

SISTER   Is that glitter?

HER   Yeah.

SISTER   Don't come to me when you haven't got any money for food because you've wasted your student loan.

HER   You've never got any money anyway.

SISTER   You don't need them.

HER   I'm going on a date.

SISTER   Right.
            I'll have some more of that. (*Indicating some prosecco.*)

HER   They'll last me years.

SISTER   I should hope so. Oh the fizz has gone up my nose.

HER   Look at you, walking around with holes in your trainers. I have to tell you they are falling apart.

SISTER   Since when did you become so judgemental? I tell you what instead of buying your spangly sparkly date-boots to attract a man why not buy me a new pair of trainers.

HER   Buy your own.

SISTER   You'll lure him in with your boots and he'll be looking at you longingly and you'll be like, Tom, Jase, Arnold –

HER   He's called Matt.

SISTER   Who?

HER   Matthew.

SISTER   Nah. Call him Arnold, you'll be like Arnold check
                out me b-gizzling jazzling spangling date-boots,
                not the only thing that b-gizzles.

HER   What are you talking about?

SISTER   I'm talking about your sparkly boots. Yeah. You'll
                be like come and get v-gizzle guzzled. How has
                that happened? Did we not buy four bottles?

                Who is this Matthew then?

                HER is looking in SISTER's stuff.

HER   Oh you know.

SISTER   What are you doing?

HER   Yeah, he's...

SISTER   Is he as boring as you?

HER   How's Johnny?

SISTER   Fine.

HER   You said you like him.

SISTER   Did I? What are you doing?

HER   What are these?

SISTER   What you doing in my stuff?

HER   You said you stopped doing these. You promised me.

SISTER   Augh.

HER   You know how you got last time.

SISTER   That was because I was doing too much last time.

HER   I'm pouring these away.

SISTER   You can give me the money for them then.

HER   When did you start taking these again?

SISTER   Oh can you please.

HER   You don't need it.

SISTER   Yeah I do. Everyone is doing it. Not everyone can
           hit all their deadlines like you.

HER   I don't hit all my deadlines.

SISTER   Well you should probably take them then. Keeps
           you up longer so you can cram more studying in.
           There is so much t t t know about. Enhances my
           performance. It's not a big deal, so just, can we
           just... have a nice evening.

HER   I was till I found out you've been lying to me.

SISTER   That's your perception of things.

           SISTER *has found the fourth bottle of prosecco
           and opens it.*

HER   She was taking more and more of the smart drug
           until she was addicted, you couldn't tell her, but
           she was. Anyone could see it. Until she started
           hallucinating and that scared her so much it made
           her stop.

           And he cancelled on me. Matt. Matthew. Blocked
           his number. Ignore him around campus and laugh
           loudly when I walk past him. I sit directly in front
           of him in lectures and I hate him.

           Spring.

           HER *twenty.* SISTER *twenty-five.*

SISTER   We are at Johnny's brother's wedding last month...
           two months ago.

HER   Johnny's got a brother?

SISTER   It was really really nice, so nice you almost think
           it's not real. Everyone was so happy.
           I'm at the bar, the father comes over.

HER   The bride's father?

SISTER   Johnny's father.

HER   You've met his parents now.

SISTER   Alcoholic. Had that smell about him. Smell it
           a mile off. Broken blood vessels all over his face,
           yellow tinge to his hair. Dirty fingernails. But all
           suited and booted with a swagger. I'll get you that
           he says, let me.
           We sit on the stools at the dark wooden bar and talk
           for a bit, and I'm thinking to myself what are you
           doing?

HER   What were you doing?

SISTER   I was at a wedding having a drink at the bar. Do you
           want to know the story or not?
           I'm sitting opposite him thinking what are you
           listening to this old man for, go and dance.
           Another drink? On me he says it's alright, I'll get
           you another one, yeah, it's not a problem, I'll get
           you that, no worries, yeah.

           So I sit there with another drink in my hand
           opposite my future father-in-law and his yellow
           eyes are all wet, and he's not happy any more and
           he's going on about regrets. About how he could
           have been a better father a better husband. I saw
           something in him, saw this pain on his face, getting
           redder as he got more animated about all the things
           he didn't do, missed opportunities. A wounded sad
           soul, broken shaken sad sad. Seething resentments
           about his ex-wife who's flaunting it with the toyboy
           she ran off with. Now this son is married and he'll
           be off, and Johnny's got me. And we should go
           over the two of us and see him more, we're more
           than welcome anytime, he pats my knee.

           He started to tell me about his daughter he'd lost
           contact with and how he misses her more than
           anything, and his eyes started to glaze and he stops
           talking and I touched his hand, surprisingly soft,
           I could feel his pain. Then he reached out. Grabbed
           my tit. Squeezed it.

More like a snake with his left hand. Didn't expect that. A room full of people.

I'd been caught off-guard. His eyes were bulging and he was smiling. Something kicked in. I got my right arm under his, my clenched fist made contact with his jaw and he went back and down, smack, and I guess he wasn't expecting that.

And I stood up, stood over him, I wanted to kick the fuck out of his face. A little crowd gathered. Johnny pushed to the front. Stopped, looked at him on the floor. Let out a little breath, hardly noticeable I only noticed because I was watching him closely waiting for him to do or say something and he lets out this little breath and looks up at me for what seemed to be like minutes. Then he laughs. Grabs my hand. Tightly. Leads me to the dance floor and we dance.

That's all I wanted to do.
He pulls me close and holds me, and I feel his warmth.
Johnny fucked me that night.
Should have been a hook with the left really.
. Should have broken his eardrum.

Pause.

HER   I'm sorry.

SISTER   Yeah.

HER   Why didn't you tell me this before?

SISTER   What would you have done?

Silence.

Can I borrow a tenner?

Movement – SISTER *chaos to euphoria.*

Summer.

HER *twenty.* SISTER *twenty-five.*

Sound of a tap running.

Movement – SISTER *slumping further and further into the floor.* HER *banging on* SISTER*'s bathroom door.*

HER   Heather will be waiting.

SISTER   I know.

HER   So why aren't you ready?

SISTER   I'm getting ready.

HER   This place is a mess.

SISTER   I'll sort it out don't don't worry.

HER   I'll wait for you.

SISTER   I don't don't want you to wait for me.

HER   When are you coming out of there?

SISTER   When I'm ready.

HER   Open the door. Open this door.

          Silence.

          SISTER *unable to hold herself up properly.*

          You look…

SISTER   What?

HER   You look –

SISTER   What?

HER   You look a mess.

SISTER   I'm fine.

HER   Yeah you look it.

SISTER   I don't want to go.

HER   Come here.

          This is supposed to be amazing look at you.

SISTER   What?

HER   Get yourself together. You're sweating. Where's your make-up?

SISTER   I haven't... I don't don't...

HER   Right come here, I'll put mine on you.

          Silence.

          HER *applies make-up to* SISTER, *who is staring back at* HER.

SISTER   I'm sorry.

          Pause.

          It'll be your graduation next year. Heather will be so proud of you.

HER   Can you stop talking.

SISTER   I'm sorry.

HER   No you're not.

          Movement – HER *in trauma.* SISTER *still.*

          Autumn.

          HER *has turned up at* SISTER's *new place with a brand-new pair of trainers in a box.*

          This is alright.

SISTER   Is it?

HER   Yeah. It's great.

SISTER   Great?

HER   It's got potential. So time of new possibilities. Did you get my keys cut?

SISTER   Not yet, no... What?

HER   I need you to close your eyes.

SISTER   What for?

HER   For me. Can you just do it? Right, don't peek. Put
               your arms out. Not like that.

               HER *places the trainer box in* SISTER*'s arms.*

               Open your eyes.

               Beat.

               Open it.

SISTER   Ah nice one.

HER   Yeah?

SISTER   Yeah nice.

HER   Got to help my sister make a good impression. For
               this afternoon.

SISTER   I'm not going.

HER   Why?

SISTER   Because I'm sick of it. Been rejected from five job
               interviews in the last month. Haven't heard
               anything back from ten others.

HER   That's part and parcel.

SISTER   When was the last time you applied for a job?

HER   I wasn't just given my job at the café just like that.

SISTER   I'm talking about a real job that I studied for.

HER   Give yourself a chance.

SISTER   I do. I try –

HER   You've been shortlisted, again.

SISTER   Why would the outcome of this sixth time be any
               different?

HER   Let me get out my crystal ball.

SISTER   Let me give you a reality check, because you are
               still cosy on your student loan and have your café
               job safe in your cocoon. It's a lot to take so much

rejection when I've just spent the past three years trying to better my prospects and it seems to not be making the blindest bit of difference.

And all the while there's still rent to be paid and food to be bought and yeah it's everyone's story, unless you've got a fucking job and you're all cosy on a Sunday afternoon in the arms of your boyfriend lying on the sofa saying oh I really don't want to go into work tomorrow and you joke about pulling a sickie and act out the phone call about food poisoning, being up all night sick. And it's all very fucking funny. Because actually you've got a job. And here I am I haven't even got a job and I've got to pretend to be well.

HER   Look I can take them back.

SISTER   I thought you bought them for me.

HER   I did.

SISTER   But only if I go to the interview? My skin is crawling. It's all been a mistake. Fuck it. The mistake that can't seem to get anything right.

HER   Why don't you just try them on?

Beat.

SISTER   It's not my fault I was a mistake.

HER   Okay.

SISTER   N'no – that's what Mum told me.

I was a mistake.
But you came along.
Definitely trying to make up for the mistake.
That was me.
Fuck it.
Don't don't know how to cope with one, but we'll have another one. Let's make it two.
So there's me, just a child looking after you a baby and looking after them the so-called parents.

She. The one who grew me inside her, from whose
womb I was dragged, nearly died. Dragged out
grappling with the air, legs and arms flailing,
fighting, premature, screaming for oxygen.
My birth nearly killed her.
She lost two litres of blood and I was five pounds
small.
Spent the first week in an incubator.
Drip-fed.
You were healthy. You were on time. You were
planned.
She even gave the shit up when she was pregnant
with you.
That saying, that parents get better with the second
child.

Beat.

HER   If you don't get this job you'll get another job, but
           if you don't go to this job you'll never know. If you
           don't go forward, what are you doing?

SISTER   It's everything getting on top of me. Doctor won't
           give me any Vali.

HER   Good.

SISTER   You don't hate yourself like I hate me you can't
           hate me more than I do already.

HER   What are you talking about? You're my favourite
           person ever.

SISTER   You're not six any more.

           I know what they all think about me. She gives me
           pregabalin. What am I a diabetic? Had to get some
           subs, two eight-mills. You could just say this is a
           pretty fucked-up existence, but then it's all deep-
           rooted in us. Monkey sees monkey does. Their
           fucked-up genes should have stopped dead with
           them. Maybe they'll stop dead with me.

Two weeks pass.

SISTER *on the up, drawing prolifically. A natural landscape, trees, a forest.*

HER   That's amazing.

SISTER   Thank you.

HER   Can I take a picture of it?

SISTER   If you like.

HER   Stand there then.

HER *takes a picture of* SISTER *on her phone.*

You like the shoes then.

SISTER   I like them more than anything ever. More than you.

HER   Thanks.

Beat.

You look good in them.

SISTER   I know. They are a bit tight but they are okay. Wear them in, you know.

HER   You're doing really well.

SISTER   I went to the park.

HER   I didn't know you go there.

SISTER   No I don't, but I just felt to. And I sat there and I looked at the trees and they looked so beautiful, I hadn't noticed before how beautiful they were. And this leaf. The green and the yellow and the red and I had to keep it. And I saw this squirrel on this branch of the tree and he had this green and red apple which was as big as half his body and I thought how the fuck did you get that apple up that tree.

Pause.

Amazing.

HER   What's the new job then?

SISTER   Just someone I know who knows my sponsor and so
           yeah when I get this job, I'll be able to, take you out
           for a meal. You won't have to cook for me all the
           time. I'm not complaining your cooking is good.

HER   Good?

SISTER   Really good.

SISTER   I'll miss it. Probably more than you.

HER   Miss what?

SISTER   I don't want to travel. The job is out of this town –
           given them my notice here. It was only ever
           temporary here anyway. Of course if I don't get it
           I'm going to have to move in with you, and then
           you can make me my breakfast and lunch as well
           as dinner.

HER   So you're moving somewhere?

SISTER   I'm not travelling to another country. Right I've got
           to go to a meeting. You can show yourself out.

           Winter.

HER   A week later she turns up on my door step. Bags
           in hand.
           She ended up staying. On my bedroom floor.
           I've been stepping over her for the past two weeks.
           I go to make my breakfast.
           I wake her up. Where are the bananas? Where are
           my bananas?

SISTER   In your cupboard, I don't know. Take someone else's.

HER   No one else has got any, there aren't any.

SISTER   You said to me I could have one. I had one. There
           was only one.

HER   If there was only one, which there wasn't, but if
           there was, my last only one, you ate it, are you
           telling me you scoffed it. Knowing it was my
           only one.

SISTER	So there was only one?
HER	No there wasn't.
SISTER	What's the big deal?
HER	What's the big deal?
SISTER	You're talking about bananas.
HER	Did you buy them? Did you reach into your pocket pull out your hard-earned cash.
SISTER	What, twenty pee.
HER	All the small things add up.
SISTER	Just get some more.
HER	I went and got them in the first place. I fancied a banana in yogurt with honey, you know when you really fancy something and you get your mind set. I go to my cupboard, thinking they'll be lovely and ripe now, but there's no bananas there. How do you think I feel?

Beat.

SISTER	You look pretty riled.

Beat.

HER	How do you think I feel?
SISTER	I thi– y– you obviously feel very upset that you couldn't get your banana and yogurt and honey, poor fucking poor fucking you. Are you going to starve to death?
HER	If it's not food it's a fiver here a tenner there.
SISTER	Oh oh oh have I bankrupt you as well?
HER	You never pay me back.
SISTER	When have I never paid you back?
HER	Only after I have begged you –

SISTER	Begged me – Oh so it's okay when you eat all my chocolate.
HER	Eat all your chocolate? What do you do own Cadbury's?
SISTER	No I don't own Cadbury's.
HER	Are you talking about your Freddo, the five-pee Freddo you gave me?
SISTER	Fifteen pee yeah.
HER	Oh fifteen pee.
SISTER	It's okay for you to eat my food?
HER	You gave it to me.
SISTER	Well next time I won't.
HER	Why is there tiny blood spots up the bathroom wall?
SISTER	I don't know, next question.
HER	Are you doing drugs in my bathroom?

Beat.

SISTER	I had a bath and I shaved my legs alright.
HER	And then you cut your leg?
SISTER	Oh yeah sorry I used your fucking razor blade is that alright?

Pause.

HER	No that's not alright.

Pause.

SISTER	Feel like… feel like…
HER	I said you could stay here if you were clean.
SISTER	I feel like everything is going to break and I feel like I'm drowning. I feel so sorry –
HER	You can't keep doing this to me.

SISTER   You're the only one who understands any of it.
            I don't know what I'd do without you.

            Movement – tender moment between the two.

            *Movement – SISTER staggering, HER watches –
            face to face they stare at each other.*

            *Movement – HER finds SISTER on her knees
            motionless – she shakes her, she stirs.*

            *Movement – HER finds SISTER slumped,
            breathing very shallow – then a big gasp –
            motionless – no pulse, overdosing. HER calls for
            an ambulance on her mobile, puts it on
            speakerphone and follows instructions from the
            call handler, giving SISTER CPR.*

HER   One two three. One two three. One two three. One
            two three. One two three. One two three. One –

SISTER   No you are harming you with whatever it is you are
            attaching to it. The idea of who you think I am and
            should be and the idea of what it makes you, as my
            sister. How people view you out there, poor you.
            Do you know how much I paid for that jacket?
            Seventy-five pounds that cost me. How dare they.
            Why did you do it? They shouldn't have done that,
            I want you to phone them up, I want I want
            compensation. I knew what I was doing I was just
            cotching, I would have been alright. They've
            ruined my clothes. Why did you let them cut my
            jacket to smithereens?

HER   Those paramedics. This young girl, younger than
            me even, she knocks on the door, I said to her,
            she's dead, I said her lips have all gone blue. She
            doesn't bat an eyelid kindly moves me out of the
            way and talks to you like a human being, and then
            another paramedic comes in and they just –

            One two three one two three one to three, nothing.
            Then they slap you. Nothing. You weren't

breathing and because you didn't have a pulse then
they cut your jacket off, to put those electrical
things on, and start on your chest, stand clear they
said and they saved your life and and you're here
and you don't seem bothered, you're not the
slightest bit grateful. They said to me if I hadn't
done what I did you wouldn't be here today. You're
one of the lucky ones. I thought you were dead.
I thought you were dead.

Silence.

SISTER   Right I'm going out, have you got a tenner?

HER   You're not going out. They told me you could
            still die.

            Movement – SISTER *going through cold turkey.*
            HER *helps and watches.*

            Movement – SISTER *struggling to stay clean and
            not use.*

            Spring.

            HER *twenty-three.* SISTER *twenty-eight.*

SISTER   What you making?

HER   We're making this.

SISTER   Wholemeal pasta?

HER   Yeah.

SISTER   Wholemeal organic handmade pasta. With what?

HER   Cheese. We are having a lot of cheese.

SISTER   Great.

HER   Can you mix that cheese. Three-cheese creamy
            sauce oh yes.

SISTER   I haven't had this for a long time.

HER   Neither have I.

SISTER	Doesn't cheese give you nightmares?
HER	No.
SISTER	Do you still get nightmares?
HER	Right is that ready?
SISTER	Haven't you seen anyone about it yet?
	It's good. It's a good thing to do.
	All Mum was good at making. Wasn't it?
HER	Hers came out of a tin.
SISTER	Oh yeah.
HER	Do you talk to your therapist about her?
SISTER	Not really.
HER	What about him?
SISTER	What about him?
HER	About our childhood.
SISTER	Sometimes. Yeah.
HER	Yeah. What do you say?
SISTER	Things like when he used to take me to the forest and we used to try and climb the oak trees. When he used to play with us.
HER	When he used to tickle us?
SISTER	Yeah I guess so.
HER	When he used to tickle us.
SISTER	I just said yeah didn't I.
HER	Where.
SISTER	What do you mean where?
HER	He used to tickle you and you'd scream and laugh and he'd laugh and put his hand up your dress or up your top and touch you.

SISTER	Why are you talking – why? Why?
HER	What about Hastings.
SISTER	What about Hastings?
HER	Remember it?
SISTER	Yeah.
HER	Remember him buying us ice cream?
SISTER	No.
HER	He bought us ice cream and he'd been holding the ice cream for so long. Sunny day. Teasing us with ice cream.
SISTER	Right.
HER	Right, and then he said we could only have our ice cream if we licked off the ice cream that had melted down his hand. And you licked his hand.
SISTER	You make shit up. I can't be round you right now, no no no I don't know why you're doing this. Why are you doing this? I thought this, I thought the macaroni cheese was because you were being –
HER	What –
SISTER	Like it was a –
HER	What –
SISTER	Thought we were making it especially.
HER	What you mean especially for my birthday?
SISTER	What?
HER	Forgotten it again.
SISTER	I don't want you coming with me. You're not laying flowers with me.
HER	And I don't want to lay flowers with you.
SISTER	I've seen Dad there.

HER	What do you mean you've seen Dad there?
SISTER	At her grave. Seen him a couple of times.
HER	Meeting up with him behind my back?
SISTER	You never come so not really.
HER	Why would you do that?
SISTER	He's still my dad.
HER	He did it to me too.
SISTER	What?
HER	What he did to you he did to me.

Silence.

I did go. She cried. I cried at the grave.

She said I want to go and pray.

We sat in the church in silence. We said nothing. We couldn't leave. She was just staring ahead with a face so sad. Then she looks me deep in the eye.

SISTER	I want to stop.
HER	Good.
SISTER	Don't know if I can on my own.
HER	You've got me. I'll stand by you, we'll see it through. It's me and you, the two of us, always has been and we're going to be okay.
SISTER	Yeah.
HER	We left the church and there he was at her grave.

Beat.

Then we sat in a pub. With our dad. The three of us sat there. He was older, I wouldn't have recognised him. Said he missed us, he said he missed her and said he was glad to see me after all this time. He's back to work, he's got someone now who apparently knows all about Mum and us. Sister sat there all the time staring at him saying nothing. He kept saying cat got your tongue. I went to the toilet came back and Dad was drenched in a pint of beer and she was standing there towering over him with a broken pint glass in her hand, threatening him. She would have glassed him if I hadn't dragged her out. Then she ran. I tried to run after her.

Movement – the release of Dad – SISTER *leaves* HER.

Movement – SISTER *cooks up –* HER *tries repeatedly to call* SISTER, *who is not picking up.*

A month later she appears, turns up on my doorstep. Banging on my door.

SISTER   I know you are there. Let me in. I want to talk to you. Let me in. I need to talk to you.

HER   I let her in.

SISTER   You've been ignoring my calls.

HER   Where have you been?

SISTER   I needed space.

HER   What do you want?

SISTER   I called you ten times today.

HER   You called me once and I was at work and when I called you back your phone was off. What do you want?

SISTER   I'm going to rehab.

HER   You're going to rehab?

SISTER   Yeah I'm pretty close.

HER   Where did you get that? (*Indicating* SISTER*'s money.*)

SISTER   I just got it. I just asked some people.

HER   Who?

SISTER	I went begging alright.
HER	Begging?
SISTER	Would you prefer I mugged someone?
HER	Why would you do that? What do you mean you went begging? Where did you go begging?
SISTER	Stop interrogating me. It was awful. I'm not proud. At least I'm being honest with you. What can I do?
HER	You begged all that?
SISTER	Of course I didn't go begging. I've borrowed a bit here and a bit there. I just needed some extra money and I'll be alright.

Beat.

HER	I haven't got it.
SISTER	I'm trying here. I'm trying to sort myself out. I thought you'd be pleased. Nah if you haven't got it respect.
HER	–
SISTER	It will be different this time yeah.
HER	Right.
SISTER	I'm changing.
HER	Yeah.
SISTER	I'm going to get clean.
HER	Okay.
SISTER	I'll pay you back. I promise.
HER	Don't do this for me.
SISTER	I'm not.
HER	Do it for you.
SISTER	I am.

HER   You have to do this.

SISTER   I am.

HER   You have to do what you say you are going to do.
            I swear this has to be the last time.

SISTER   I promise.

HER   I close the door. I love with fear.

            Movement – SISTER *shoots up. Goes back to* HER
            two days later.

SISTER   No I was just doing it one last time to get me to
            rehab, to get me through, get me ready, to say
            goodbye. It was a tiny bit. Hardly did anything.

HER   This is Mum all over again.

SISTER   I'm not Mum.

HER   I think I'm falling apart. I don't think I can...

SISTER   I'm not like her. I can stop. And now I'm ready I'm
            going to detox.

HER   You can't do it here.

SISTER   No I know. I'm booked in. I met someone in the
            rooms, they are helping me out.

HER   I'll take you there.

            She drinks cans of fizzy drinks the whole way
            there, lying on the back seat of my car, hardly says
            a word.

            We get there, in the white waiting room we sit for
            ages and get called in to see a doctor. She says she
            really wants to get off it, this time. I cry. He says she
            can't take anything in, mobile, jewellery, money.
            She will be out of it for most of it. We hug. She
            follows a nurse out. I look at the doctor, his head in
            his paperwork. She'll be okay he says. I leave.

Summer.

HER *twenty-five*. SISTER *twenty-eight*.

HER   In six weeks I come back to get her and she's a
        different person, her skin is glowing. And she's off
        it, she's clean, I feel hope. She has nowhere to stay
        and so comes back to me, and for a while, for two
        weeks exactly it's okay.

        You've been doing really well.

SISTER It was shit, everyone was bang at it, the place was
        a dump. The room had a plastic shiny floor, a
        greyish yellow. Peach-coloured painted walls.
        White ceiling, smoke alarm, metal round light with
        glass front looking down from the centre of the
        ceiling onto the bed, I think it had a camera in it.

HER   It wouldn't have had a camera in it.

SISTER Were you there? Small table with a drawer to the
        left. Old armchair with plastic pink covering,
        wardrobe to the right. On an old small desk with one
        drawer a TV and you know what's funny it had the
        remote, the same remote that was smacked across
        my head when you begged and begged and begged
        Mum that time. I can't get away from any of it.

        What did you think it was going to be like?

HER   Sorry.

SISTER For what? What you sorry for? You thought that
        was just going to cure me – then and there, but
        there's other shit to deal with now, and other shit
        has come back up. Maybe we should just step back
        from each other for a bit. You know. Because now
        I'm a bit…

        Coming off of benzos was the worst. I haven't
        slept, can't remember the last time. So I've gone
        and got myself some mirtazapine, and I'm on
        happy pills and am I fucking happy? Do you know

what one of the side effects is, sui– fucking suicide.
I should have just stayed on it.

HER   No you shouldn't.

SISTER   To top it all I'm supposed to look after a plant, get
          a plant or a pet.
          Fucking... So, I mean you've been great, I'm going
          to just try now. On my own.
          For a bit.
          Have a bit of space.

HER   Hello.

SISTER   Don't fucking ever call me again.

HER   What do you want?

SISTER   Where are you?

HER   I'm out.

SISTER   Out, out where exactly?

HER   What do you want?

SISTER   Hope you're having a lov– lovely great evening,
          having a wonderful life, out out out and about.

HER   What did you want?

SISTER   It doesn't matter now. It's not important any more.

HER   Obviously it was important – to call me six times.

SISTER   It's nothing. I wouldn't have h h had to if you hada
          had of picked up first time. You're supposed to be
          there for me.

HER   I'm having a night off from you.

SISTER   I thought there was something wrong.

HER   You're just trying to tap me up for money. You
          think I don't have a life.

SISTER   Well you must do because you are out and about
          somewhere.

HER   Having a nice time and I've just left / to call you
             back so what do you want?

SISTER   You haven't left, I can hear you're still there. Why
             are you lying?

HER   Don't like how it feels?

SISTER   You said you would be watching this programme
             but you're obviously not so I can't talk to you
             about it and there's another programme on the
             other side and if you were watching the TV you
             would have seen it.

HER   What programme?

SISTER   It doesn't matter. It doesn't matter now, I'm in bed
             and I have nothing to say to you and you have
             nothing to say to me so what's the point.

HER   I didn't say I would be watching anything –

SISTER   Don't get it twisted. I haven't fucking finished yet.
             You said you'd be watching it, don't get it twisted
             even if you said you were watching something
             I wouldn't expect you to be really watching it –

HER   I'm putting the phone down on you –

SISTER   I let you say your shit. Don't get it twisted. Don't
             fucking ever fucking call me again. Fuck off out of
             my life.

HER   Turns out she was on a concoction of pills and
             alcohol. When I got home she was lying on my
             doorstep.

             Two weeks later.

             I need to know you'll be okay.

SISTER   Of course I'll be okay.

HER   Nick has got a new job –

SISTER   Good for Nick.

HER   And he's moving with work and he's asked me to
           go with him. So I'll be moving and you'll have to
           find somewhere –

SISTER   Find somewhere?

HER   You won't be able to stay here.

SISTER   You might have a problem.

HER   What?

SISTER   You can't move my friends. It's pointless.

HER   If I block up their nest / the mother will take them
           away.

SISTER   Drey. Birds have nests, squirrels have dreys. You're
           not driving them away. You will get done if you
           release them back into the wild.

HER   They – how – I can't – I don't understand you.

SISTER   They like it here. Space for them to run. George
           was hiding once, found him in your – you know
           that – bag, the one with the big brushes –

HER   I might get rabies.

SISTER   More likely mad-squirrel disease. You might be
           infected now, it might have seeped into your pores
           and infiltrating your grey matter, and your brains
           might just explode everywhere.

HER   I'm driving them out before –

SISTER   How are you driving them out if you are blocking
           up every hole you find.

HER   It's a precaution until the rodent-control people
           come round.

SISTER   You wouldn't dare.

HER   They are vermin, rodents.

SISTER   You'll never make them move on, they like it here,
           they are too intelligent for you, even a baby would
           be too intelligent for you.

HER *is rooting through a cupboard, finds a broom.*

What you doing?

HER   I am going to find them and smash them.

SISTER   You smash them and I'll smash you.

HER   Yeah?

SISTER   Yeah. They're mine, you you don't don't even you
              never you think you think you're something you've
              got you – live in this place and you – anything I've
              got, anything I, anything – and you – always –
              I can't even move – What are you looking at?

HER   Your dark eyes.

SISTER   Do you remember her face when we found her?

HER   I told you –

SISTER   Constantly reliving the moment in my mind. It just
              won't –

HER   Stop.

SISTER   You don't know what it's like.

HER   I was there remember.

SISTER   Remember you thought it was a trick, you thought
              it was a game me and her had concocted. Sleeping
              Lions. You thought I'd do that to you.

HER   You're sick if you think that.

SISTER   I think you wanted them all to yourself.

HER   That's not true and you know it.

SISTER   She was a twat. She fucked up my whole life.

HER   One minute you feel sorry for her and the next
              she's the reason you're the way you are.

SISTER   I do feel sorry for her. It poisoned her brain then
              claimed her life.

Didn't know where I stood from one minute to
the next.
Doped up to her eyeballs most of the time, dead in
the eyes, pinprick eyes.

HER   Or drinking cheap cider.

SISTER   Nasty stuff like five-cans-for-a-pound nasty.

HER   Yeah.

SISTER   She may as well have been dead.
            Deteriorating from the inside, shutting down.
            A wreck on the outside, puking up.
            Wish I had have killed her.
            Mum, at school today guess we what we –
            Nothing
            Mum, do you like my picture?

HER   I remember that.

SISTER   Nothing.
            Blank stare.

            Never showed her a picture since.

HER   Your artwork is great.

SISTER   Yeah.
            Screaming matches. Smashing things up.
            A pretty fucked-up existence –

HER   But we had each other.

SISTER   We do.
            But it's all deep-rooted in us.
            Monkey sees monkey does.

HER   Screaming, shouting, squabbling slagging matches.

SISTER   Adrenalin surging through me. Feeling alive.

HER   Feeling something.

SISTER   Feeling something. You just used to bellow and
            bawl till you were blue in the face. When you

wanted that yellow teddy bear, begged her, begged
her, begged her, till you were blue in the face, told
her you would jump out of your bedroom window
if she didn't get it for you.

HER   Yeah.

SISTER   Had the back of her slipper right across my face.
The weight behind the smack of a hard rubber sole.
Split my lip.
Bright-red mark across my jaw.

HER   That wasn't my –

SISTER   No? I had a remote – television remote smacked
across my head, when you were begging her for
your programme.
Broke it.
She couldn't change a channel after that, served
her right.

HER   I love you.

           I want you to be happy.

SISTER   Why? Because that's what I deserve?

HER   I want to be happy.

SISTER   Because that's what life should be? We should all
be happy people walking about with big silly
smiles on our faces all day every day.

HER   That's not what –

SISTER   Be grateful when we wake up and put our feet on
the floor and say thank you, thank you, thank you
world for this day, thank you universe for my life.
I'm so grateful. I'm so happy. I'm so full of the
joys of spring I could burst with happiness.

HER   It would be nice to have some fucking happiness
wouldn't it.
I'm sick of this. I'm fucking sick of this.

SISTER   I could have left you but I didn't. When we went to Heather's and I turned nineteen, they asked me if I wanted to leave, that I could leave if I wanted to and I said no I will stay for my baby sister, my fourteen-year-old baby sister wouldn't be able to cope without me. Because she never has and never will because she's always been a baby. The planned baby that everyone wanted. The baby that threw tantrums until she got her teddy, got her dresses –

HER and SISTER embrace. After a while HER tries to break free but SISTER doesn't let go. They grapple. HER breaks free and falls to the floor. SISTER towers over HER. They stare at each other for a long time.

Winter.

HER *twenty-three.* SISTER *twenty-eight.*

HER   And again she went to rehab. Full three months this time. Stuck it out. We didn't see each other the whole time. Got more help myself. Gave me space to... be with myself and... didn't know... what to do with myself... breathe... start looking at my part in all of it. Big changes had to – the possibility of – I would stick to – be made and stuck to. Promises... unbroken. Tough love.

She looked great this time. Healthy. I thought this is it now. And I felt great. Proud of her. She'd got a new place, I'd found somewhere new to live with Nick. Everything was changing.

So that night, Friday night, Nick and I had our last night together in this town.

He's great. We were having a lovely evening.

Lying there in his arms, never felt so safe before, warm, his legs wrapped over mine, his chest beating and all of a sudden this fear swept through my mind, I couldn't move, this tension in my chest. I gasped

for air. I had to get out of there. I couldn't breathe.
I just left, two o'clock in the morning I left.

Through the town straight past a crowd outside the
pub I last saw my dad, past a chalkboard saying
'happy hour two-for-one'.

Past the Chinese takeaway with its steamed-up
windows and lucky cat. Waving with one paw.
Tried calling my sister, twenty times.

Got to her front door. Banging on her front door.
Banging on the windows. Got her keys out of my
bag, dropped the keys, picked them up thought that
the door needed a lick of paint as I opened it.

There she is on the floor. Sitting there. Tapping on
the syringe. Belt in her mouth. She looks directly at
me. She shoots up in front of me. The needle
sticking in her arm, getting off her head.

Silence.

SISTER   I promise –

HER   You look…

SISTER   I promise –

HER   Amazing.

SISTER   I promise – This is the last time.

HER   You're floating.

SISTER   This time is the last time.

SISTER   Go back…

HER   What?

SISTER   In the woods, in the trees…

HER   Body slumping.

SISTER   They scuttle…

HER   Eyes closing.

SISTER   Scamper…

HER   Mouth opening.

SISTER   Jump about…

HER   Life draining away.

SISTER   Race about. Up to the top… of the treetops, upside
            down, they fly about. All three rolled into one that's
            me, jumping…

HER   I can't do this.

SISTER   I'm running.

HER   Yes.

SISTER   Flying.

HER   If their breathing changes and they are turning
            blue.

            I know it's a matter of minutes. I know where the
            naloxone syringe is.

            What happens if I don't get it?

            I'm stopped with shock stock-still in my tracks at
            my own thoughts.
            Heart slowing slowly poisoned polluted.

            I'm sorry I couldn't make it any better.
            You were a beautiful mistake.
            We'll be free.

            HER *watches* SISTER *in silence*.

            A flash of light like a lighter flame then

            Blackout.

A Nick Hern Book

Poisoned Polluted first published in Great Britain in 2019 as a paperback original by Nick Hern Books Limited, The Glasshouse, 49a Goldhawk Road, London W12 8QP

Cover photograph by Nick Rutter; design by Nick Thompson

Designed and typeset by Nick Hern Books, London
Printed in Great Britain by Mimeo Ltd, Huntingdon, Cambridgeshire PE29 6XX

A CIP catalogue record for this book is available from the British Library

ISBN 978 1 84842 918 5

www.nickhernbooks.co.uk

facebook.com/nickhernbooks

twitter.com/nickhernbooks